Arctic Animals
Life Outside the Igloo

Arctic Fox

by Dee Phillips

Consultants:

Alysa McCall, Field Programs Manager
Polar Bears International, Winnipeg, Manitoba, Canada

Kimberly Brenneman, PhD
National Institute for Early Education Research, Rutgers University, New Brunswick, New Jersey

BEARPORT
PUBLISHING

New York, New York

Credits

Cover, © Steven J. Kazlowski/Alamy; 2–3, © outdoorsman/Shutterstock; 4–5, © Michio Hoshino/Minden Pictures/FLPA; 7T, © Alex Uralsky/Shutterstock; 7B, © Tony Campbell/Shutterstock; 8, © Michael Gore/FLPA; 9, © John Pitcher/Istockphoto; 10, © age fotostock/Superstock; 11, © Incredible Arctic/Shutterstock; 12T, © J.L. Klein and M.L. Hubert/FLPA; 12B, © Sergey Gorshkov/Minden Pictures/FLPA; 13, © Sergey Gorshkov/Minden Pictures/FLPA; 14, © Ignacio Yufera/FLPA; 15, © Incredible Arctic/Shutterstock; 16, © Incredible Arctic/Shutterstock; 17, © Tom Brakefield/Superstock; 18T, © Sergey Gorshkov/Minden Pictures/FLPA; 18B, © Jasper Doest/Minden Pictures/FLPA; 19, © Jasper Doest/Minden Pictures/FLPA; 20, © Sergey Gorshkov/Minden Pictures/FLPA; 21, © Sergey Gorshkov/Minden Pictures/FLPA; 22, © hagit berkovich/Shutterstock, © Paul Reeves Photography/Shutterstock, © Vibe Images/Shutterstock, and © Cynthia Kidwell/Shutterstock; 23TC, © Tony Campbell/Shutterstock; 23TR, © ecoventurestravel/Shutterstock; 23BL, © Jasper Doest/Minden Pictures/FLPA; 23BR, © Ignacio Yufera/FLPA.

Publisher: Kenn Goin
Creative Director: Spencer Brinker
Editor: Jessica Rudolph
Photo Researcher: Ruby Tuesday Ltd

Library of Congress Cataloging-in-Publication Data

Phillips, Dee, 1967–
  Arctic fox / by Dee Phillips.
    pages cm. — (Arctic animals)
  Includes bibliographical references and index.
  ISBN 978-1-62724-530-2 (library binding) — ISBN 1-62724-530-8 (library binding)
  1. Arctic fox—Juvenile literature. I. Title.
  QL737.C22P488 2014
  599.776'4—dc23
                        2014036567

For more information, write to Bearport Publishing Company, Inc., 45 West 21st Street, Suite 3B, New York, New York 10010. Printed in the United States of America.

10 9 8 7 6 5 4 3 2 1

Contents

Hungry Foxes

It's a winter morning in the **Arctic**.

Two fluffy, white arctic foxes walk across the snow.

The foxes are following a polar bear that is on the hunt.

If the bear catches a seal, there will be leftovers for the foxes to eat.

The hungry foxes are careful not to get too close to the huge bear, though.

They don't want to become a meal themselves!

An arctic fox is about the size of a small dog. An adult fox can be 27 inches (69 cm) long from its nose to its rear end.

polar bear

arctic fox

How would you describe the
foxes' Arctic home to someone
who has never seen it?

An Arctic Fox's World

The arctic fox's home is one of the coldest places on Earth.

In the Arctic, freezing winds blow, and temperatures can drop to –40°F (–40°C).

For most of the year, the rocky land is covered with ice and snow.

The weather is so cold that part of the ocean surface freezes over.

How do you think arctic foxes keep warm in the cold weather?

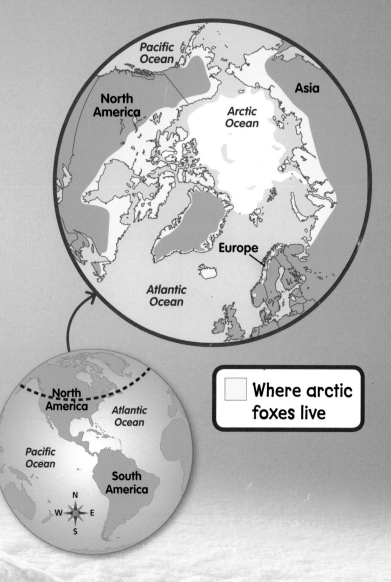

Pacific Ocean

North America

Asia

Arctic Ocean

Europe

Atlantic Ocean

North America

Atlantic Ocean

Pacific Ocean

South America

N
W   E
S

☐ Where arctic foxes live

During summer, temperatures in the Arctic warm up a little. Then the ice and snow melt, and plants are able to grow.

summer in the Arctic

an arctic fox in winter

A Coat for Winter

In fall, an arctic fox grows a coat of thick, white fur.

The fur keeps the little fox from getting cold.

A fox's white coat is also good **camouflage.**

The animal blends in with its snowy and icy world.

This helps the fox hide from wolves and polar bears that want to eat it.

an arctic fox blending in with the snow

In summer, the ice and snow melt. How do you think arctic foxes stay hidden from enemies at this time of year?

An arctic fox has a long, furry tail called a "brush." The fox curls its brush around its face just like a scarf. This helps it keep warm.

furry brush

9

A Coat for Summer

In spring, an arctic fox's white coat starts to shed, or fall out.

At the same time, the fox grows a new brownish-gray coat.

This summer coat is also good camouflage.

It helps the fox blend in with the rocks and plants.

Once again, the little fox is able to stay hidden from its enemies.

An arctic fox's summer coat is thinner than its winter coat. The thin coat keeps the fox from getting too warm when the temperature rises.

an arctic fox blending in with its rocky world

11

Going Hunting

All year, arctic foxes hunt animals such as lemmings and voles.

In winter, these tiny creatures dig tunnels and live under the snow.

To catch a lemming, a fox listens carefully until it hears the animal moving around.

Then it leaps into the air and dives into the snow.

In an instant, it grabs the lemming in its mouth.

a lemming hiding under the snow

an arctic fox diving into the snow

a fox grabbing a lemming

Arctic foxes also eat seabirds, eggs, fish, insects, berries—and even the poop of other animals!

A Fox Den

Adult arctic foxes usually live in pairs.

In early spring, a male and a female fox will **mate**.

The two foxes dig a home, called a **den**, beneath some rocks.

They make tunnels and small rooms.

The foxes use the rooms for resting and storing food.

a pair of arctic foxes in spring

den entrance

In summer, when there is lots of food around, foxes bring extra food into their den. They eat this stored food in winter.

Family Time

About eight weeks after mating, a mother fox gives birth.

The mother and her babies, called pups, are safe and cozy in their underground home.

The tiny foxes drink milk from their mother's body.

The father fox goes hunting and brings back food for the mother fox to eat.

an arctic fox father carrying a bird

arctic fox pup

A mother arctic fox usually gives birth to a **litter** of about five pups. However, she might give birth to as many as 20 pups.

A Growing Family

When the pups are three weeks old, their mother leaves them alone.

She goes out hunting, just like the father fox.

The little pups wait for their parents at the entrance to the den.

The parent foxes bring food back to the pups.

The babies eat some meat, but they still drink milk, too.

pups waiting at the den entrance

a pup eating a bird

In July or August, the mother fox gives birth to a second litter of babies. Now the parent foxes have even more pups to care for!

mother arctic fox

How do you think arctic fox pups learn to hunt?

a pup drinking milk

19

The Fox Pups Grow Up

As each day passes, the pups grow bigger and stronger.

They learn how to hunt by watching their mother and father.

By the time they are three months old, each pup can hunt for itself.

When they are ten months old, the young foxes leave their parents.

The grown-up arctic foxes will soon start families of their own.

a pup practicing hunting

Science Lab

All About the Dog Family

Arctic foxes are members of the dog, or canine, family—just like fennec foxes, red foxes, gray wolves, and coyotes.

Choose one of the dog family members shown below and then use books and the Internet to research how it lives.

Next, make a chart to compare and contrast the life of an arctic fox with the animal you've chosen.

An arctic fox and a fennec fox

Things that are the same	Things that are different
Arctic fox and fennec fox mothers feed their babies milk.	Arctic foxes live in the freezing Arctic, while fennec foxes live in hot deserts.
Arctic foxes and fennec foxes live in dens.	Arctic foxes have small ears, while fennec foxes have huge ears.

fennec fox   red fox   gray wolf   coyote

Science Words

Arctic (ARK-tik) the northernmost area on Earth, which includes the Arctic Ocean and the North Pole

camouflage (KAM-uh-flazh) colors and markings that help an animal blend in with its surroundings

den (DEN) a home where wild animals can rest, be safe, and have babies

litter (LIT-ur) a group of animals born to the same mother at the same time

mate (MAYT) to come together in order to have young

23

Index

Read More

Marsico, Katie. *Arctic Fox (A Day in the Life: Polar Animals).* Chicago, IL: Heinemann Library (2012).

Owen, Ruth. *Arctic Fox Pups (Wild Baby Animals).* New York: Bearport (2011).

Sisk, Maeve T. *Arctic Foxes (Animals That Live in the Tundra).* New York: Gareth Stevens (2011).

Learn More Online

To learn more about arctic foxes, visit **www.bearportpublishing.com/ArcticAnimals**

About the Author

Dee Phillips lives near the ocean on the southwest coast of England. She develops and writes nonfiction and fiction books for children of all ages.